CO-ABP-269

THESE

Contributors

ELIZABETH BOWEN
RHYS DAVIES
RUMER GODDEN
ALDOUS HUXLEY
ELIZABETH JANEWAY
JOSEPH WOOD KRUTCH
AUBREY MENEN
MARIANNE MOORE
DOM MORAES
ALAN PRYCE-JONES
SANTHA RAMA RAU

SIMPLE THINGS

Some Appreciations of

the Small Joys in Daily Life

from HOUSE & GARDEN

Simon and Schuster   New York

PS
688
.H6

10/29/65 Eastin 2.30

ALL RIGHTS RESERVED
INCLUDING THE RIGHT OF REPRODUCTION
IN WHOLE OR IN PART IN ANY FORM
COPYRIGHT © 1962, 1963, 1965
BY THE CONDÉ NAST PUBLICATIONS INC.
PUBLISHED BY SIMON AND SCHUSTER, INC.
ROCKEFELLER CENTER, 630 FIFTH AVENUE
NEW YORK 20, N. Y.

SECOND PRINTING

LIBRARY OF CONGRESS CATALOG CARD NUMBER: 65-15023
MANUFACTURED IN THE UNITED STATES OF AMERICA
BY H. WOLFF BOOK MFG. CO., N. Y.
DESIGNED BY EDITH FOWLER

49777

ǂFA

CONTENTS

The pleasure we find in the multiplicity of things around us depends entirely on our awareness of them. If our perceptions are lively and our senses on the alert, we don't need to be told we are happy. But if they have fallen asleep, we might as well be destitute. To wake up our senses, the editors of *House & Garden* decided a few years ago to make a new scrutiny of the older, simpler, humbler things about us—"the little things," as the poet Rilke defined them, "that can so unexpectedly become big and beyond measuring."

To that end, we commissioned some of the finest contemporary writers in English—men and women, poets, novelists, playwrights, essayists, natives of three continents—to set down the thoughts and emotions stirred

9

in them by the common tools and utensils, the elemental foods and materials that go so often unseen, unvalued, unenjoyed. The result was a collection of perceptive, heart-warming, illuminating essays, which appeared in eleven consecutive issues of *House & Garden*. Now that they have been collected in this volume, we hope that you will enjoy them as much as we did and will reread them often.

—HARRIET BURKET
Editor-in-Chief

THE TEAKETTLE

ELIZABETH BOWEN

When I begin to speak of the teakettle, all, but *all*, of my friends exclaim, "You mean teapot!" Thus is the noble, necessary kettle slighted. Virtually, it is unknown to history; poetry's tributes to it have been niggardly; seldom has it posed for its portrait. Sadly few kettles are in museums—to the kettle's past has gone (I find) but little research. Meanwhile the teapot, that famous beauty, revels in every kind of publicity. Skills of every kind have gone to adorn it—it has succeeded in being everything, from classical-type to romantic-pretty, from aristocratic-looking to good and cozy. At one time, the teapot aped the form of a wine vase; at the other extreme, Cubism took it

over (not, it has been agreed, with the best results).
Apart from favorite teapots in daily use, many are
singled out to be sheer ornaments.

The background kettle goes into the pot-and-pan
class.

Yet, where would the teapot be without the teakettle? Nowhere. What would the teapot be without the
teakettle? In effect, nothing.

The sapient and civilized Chinese grasped those
two verities fairly early—tea-making being among the
arts they first pioneered in, then perfected. It was in
the eighth century A.D. that the Chinese made their
epoch-making discovery—i.e., that one does not boil
tea; one infuses it. For that, what is necessary? Boiling water. Repeat, boiling—water right *at* the boil.
How best should that reach the tea leaves without
(on the way) exposure to cooling air? Down a spout.
How was escape of heat (in the form of steam)
through the open top of the vessel to be prevented?
By the addition of a lid.

The ingenious eighth-century Chinese therefore at
once designed, and put into use, a small tea-water
kettle. On the chafing dish principle, this had beneath

it a portable charcoal burner. This was (I have ascertained) the first known teakettle. The English were slow to profit by that particular wisdom of the Orient's; tea itself having reached them in the seventeenth century, they became from then on increasingly fervent addicts. They continued to boil tea-water in sloppy cauldrons—enterprise with regard to tea taking the form, chiefly, of heavy smuggling, to evade the sky-high tariffs.

More or less exactly 1,000 years after the teakettle notion had dawned on China, it at last found favor with English genius. The teakettle, once it began to be made in England, developed an English style of its own. Sturdy in outline, it had an ample base. Destined to be perched upon stoked-up coal fires, it needed to be resistant to their heat—accordingly, it was wrought of the stoutest metals: iron or copper. Smoke soon blackened, soot caked, its veteran surface. And, although it had a handle above its lid, near *that* dared venture no human hand! To shift or lift such a kettle, one used a pothook.

How unlike its dainty Chinese progenitor! Our teakettle, grimed by hard years, was rated accordingly.

Thankless treatment rewarded it, often, for faithful service. Nonetheless, this tribe maintained an *élite* —slenderer, shinier kettles—which fared better.

Delightful as may be the shape, glaze, porcelain florals, gilt swags, cameo profiles, bird or scenery motifs, or all or any decorative medallions upon the teapot, without the teakettle there can be no tea. The teapot, for all its charms, is a sheer dependent. The chubbiest, homiest-looking brown glazed earthenware teapot is—as to this—one with its ornate sister. The brown teapot, with its realist farmhouse ancestry, does not (be certain) kid itself as to that. The fragile porcelain teapot has learned humility. The antique silver variant is no fool, either—whether upright Queen Anne, curved Georgian, fluted Regency or rotund Victorian. The teakettle, nominal servitor to the teapot, does, in actual fact, play the master role.

That axiom is instilled into all true tea-makers. Tea-making's whole, old lore concentrates in one saying: "You bring the Pot to the Kettle; you *don't* bring the Kettle to the Pot!" Why? Because, not more than a split second must elapse between the lifting of the now-at-the-boil kettle from the flame and the tilting of the still-at-the-boil water on to the tea leaves waiting (inside the waiting teapot) to be infused. Moreover, the teapot will have been scalded prior to the spooning in of the tea leaves, else the "bite" of the boilingness of the water might be reduced. The iniquity of bringing to the kettle a teapot with coldness in it is very great.

The teakettle summons the teapot at its psychic, own, imperative moment. That we should require the ear-splitting "whistling" kettle to blare forth that moment shows (*I* think) some decline—should the kettle-lover not recognize what is happening by means of some tuned and alert sense? The kettle first "sings" (that, poetry *has* allowed it!) then approaches the boil at noisy crescendo. Once at the boil, it changes its rhythm. The steam's fierce sibilance is what is chiefly, now, to be heard. Air vibrates, startled, at the mouth of the spout.

What a drama. What a dramatic contrast with the actual, timeless calmness of *drinking* tea.

Long gone, the formal tea-hour once spun its magic. There was an element, also, of ceremonial, Oriental-descended, not inappropriate. English country houses (of which the greater survive as viewable "stately homes") set up a special mystique with regard to "tea." That word stood for far, far more than the beverage. "Tea," in fact, was a high, a drawing-room occasion: some ladies dressed for it specially—hence, the "tea-gown." Observant (and imitative), the French preferred to call this occasion *"le five-o' clock."* And then it was that the teakettle, along with the teapot, enjoyed full limelight. In sailed the two heavenly twins, of silver, resplendent, borne on a silver tray. The tray came to rest on a low but abundant table—whereon "iced" cakes, ethereal pastries, "hot cakes" (liquid with butter), delicate sandwiches, petal-thin bread-and-butter waited, set out on a lacy cloth. Flocks of teacups looked like a *corps de ballet.* Any hostess of worth insisted (although there were servitors) on going through with "making the tea" herself—as audience, her guests. The kettle and teapot were, it must be stated, non-identical twins, for the former was elevated some three to four inches on its silver tripod, within which pulsed a spirit-blue flame. An essential attendant, naturally, was the tea caddy, silver as they come, with its little scoop. The kettle, it need hardly be said, required not more than a lick from the small blue flame. The drawing-room-entering kettle contained water already brought to the boil, off-stage. A caked old black kitchen kettle had, very probably, done the work.

For all their grand style, all their polished paraphernalia, those long-vanished drawing-room tea hours were far from freezing ones. "The cup that cheers, but not inebriates," is—*I* feel, always—a line written with more than an impish smile. The drinking of tea sets up an inebriation of its own. It was, in fact, denounced by furious puritans, than which a greater tribute could hardly be. Talk around those glittering tea tables (one may gather, from the reading of any period memoirs) had a peculiar, relaxed but racy, above all intimate flavor. Gossip, glancing confidences and charming if perilous innuendo flourished no less when unheated by alcohol. From those rosy or turquoise cups, with their frilled gilt lips, *what* insidious aroma came floating up?

It floats up still—changed though the scene is. Endlessly, now more casual, the set-out of tea engenders the ancient magic—to which are added less of the perils, more of the sweetnesses of intimacy. Here still, *still*, is an hour like no other! Gently social—when it is social at all: ideally an hour for two, for dear friends. An hour, even, for the solitary, who drawing her small tea tray alongside her big chair, turns her lamp on her book, preparing to sip and read. But, does she read? May she not find herself musing on other tea hours? In the other big chair, opposite, has she not perhaps an imaginary companion —someone who was there yesterday, will be there tomorrow, or who through the very fact that he cannot be there again will be there always?

Tea can be drunk in the garden; that is lovely. It can be drunk in a big bay window outside which sweet-smelling spring rain is falling. But I think the ideal tea is drunk by the fire. And does not fire call up a rotund presence, singing, still-languidly steaming, upon the hob? (Hob, *yes*: though where are those hobs now?) Dear kettle, wherever you work, however you boil—circular gas flame, plugged-in electricity or the wavering spirit-stove—I love you.

Thank you for tea. Without you, there could be none.

THE KNIFE

MARIANNE MOORE

I have a knife held by two nails flat to the casing of my kitchen china closet. It has a blade about eight inches long, of high-grade steel, joined to an ebony handle by a collar of brass—trade-marked Encore, Thomas Turner, Cutler to His Majesty—bought in Oxford in 1911 for cutting bread and cheese, by my mother and me who had lodgings in Magpie Lane, formerly Grove Street, not far from the Bodleian. Up a flight of stairs, above the reading room of the Library, among the exhibition cases containing objects congruous with the interests of studious persons, were trenchers on one of which the motto said,

> *If thou be young then marry not yet.*
> *If thou be olde, then no wife get*
> *For young men's wives will not be taught*
> *And olde men's wives be good for naught.*

I think this motto may have had a part in my dislike of the reversed order of words in verse which purports to be poetry.

My Turner knife is so sharp as to tempt use for cutting more than bread—for sectioning grapefruit, for slicing a lemon, a watermelon; for freeing honeycomb that has cemented itself almost permanently to the frame. The result: stains which indict hands too hurried to scour a knife with steel glow or Bon Ami —indication of housewifely status, as indisputable as the diamonds and rubies encrusting the massive gold swords provided by the King for each fairy invited to the Christening of his daughter, the Princess, in Perrault's story of "The Sleeping Beauty."

A massive gold sword, as a paper knife, however, is less practical than tortoise shell, ivory, or the steel desk knife made by certain German manufacturers with a Mercury's head on the hilt and the word Victory. Metal is of course no match esthetically for the beveled ebony Japanese paper cutter sold by Takahashi in San Francisco; or for a Chinese ivory paper knife of the kind once given me—the handle diminishing in diameter from a short neatly rounded animal tail which appears to dive through the ivory from one side, while nose and ears come through on the other. Ivory seems the best edge for India paper— rather than a crazy sharp edge which could veer into the margin, or tear a corner off diagonally.

Yes, a knife is essential. As Admiral Roscoe F. Good observed, "A seafaring man without a knife is no sailor."

For correspondents with a security complex, who seal a flap shut to the last vestige of gummed edge, a tiny shop in Venice has exactly the blade: Ferigo Andrea, Cottelleria Arrotinaria, S. Marco 2358 Calle delle Ostreghe. The case of white bone is $1\frac{1}{16}$ inches long, secured by three brass rivets, with a red dot near the hinge. The blade, with thumb groove, has a ring and a point fine enough to enter an opening the size of a pinpoint. With a paper clip attached to the ring, this "bino" (*bambino*) need not be mislaid.

The shop regards skinning knives as its specialty, but it has also a fruit knife and two-pronged fork of stainless steel, each with white composition handle. Using these as a substitute for the gigantic implements afforded by ships and hotels, one may rival the waiter paring a hard peach or apple without resting a finger on the part one would eat. I bought the pair; then was presented soon after with a Greek knife which has a two-inch steel blade in a two-inch grip, the blade engraved with a four-petaled flower on one side and on the other a fish carrying away a bit of fish-line. Symmetrically warted by rivet heads that stabilize the blade, the brass handle of the knife has *repoussé* circles enclosing three small paste jewels—what appears to be a bloodstone between two garnets.

In size but not charm, my Greek flat sword is surpassed, naturally, by the watermelon knife which dominated the account by P. Papakoukas in the Athens *News* from the city's midsummer "watermelon front," which went more or less as follows:

"I once again deal with the so easily wielded instrument which these days has reached a peak of activity. Two watermelon sellers got angry with a customer who didn't find the sliced watermelon red enough, and treated him like a watermelon awaiting the knife.

Every summer the color of this delicious fruit creates a multitude of misunderstandings which culminate in the police precinct. The scene is something like this: the watermelon seller with his pushcart . . . the innocent customer.

'Are they red?'

'If they're not, you don't take any. . . .' And the knife flashes forth. . . . 'Fire couldn't be redder.'

'It's not red.'

'Not red?'

An argument follows as to which is color blind. . . . At times experts are called in. . . . 'Excuse me, sir. Please, one minute of your time. . . . Is this watermelon red?' In about three minutes twenty experts gather, each shouting an opinion.

'It's red.'

'No, it isn't, it's pink.'

'White.'

'Twenty years I've been selling watermelon and I know what I'm saying.'

'I have been eating watermelons for forty years. . . .'

'Since I cut it, you have to buy it.'

'If it isn't a watermelon but a marrow, what'll I do with it? Give it to the chickens? . . .'

'You're a marrow yourself . . . look like one.'

There is no need for all this. Let the guessing as to the color be a question of technique, luck and extra-sense perception. . . . A police order on the matter could settle it once and for all."

We say he that lives by the sword shall die by the sword. The Roman, the Florentine and the Etruscan were not convinced of this. Could any warrior surpass in might an Etruscan holding up a 40-pound shield and long sword, under a helmet four or five feet long from crest to caudal tip? Giorgione's "A Soldier," in crimson, sword vertical, facing forward like a magistrate or philosopher, implies the opposite of bloodshed. Votes against Hippocrates when nom-

inated for exile were never sufficient to exile him, as
the count by *ostrakon* in Athens' Museum of the
Agora shows. Fragments and little implements found
where Phidias had his shop at Olympia as well as
Charcot's triumph of surgery belong to the mythology of skill in which creative imagination (say, the
soul) dwarfs any instance of triumph in combat.

That Praxiteles' Hermes should seem from the left
to smile and from the right to ponder, baffles analy-
sis. Marble cutting, manually, is becoming a lost art;
as demonstrated in Michelangelo's David and in the
Moses which was to be part of the tomb of Pope
Julius II. The Moses—to the right of the chains
which bound the Apostle Peter in the church named
for him, San Pietro in Vincoli—is another proof that
sculptors of saints are too often obstructed by un-
saintly contemporaries. For the quarrymen of Car-
rara by their cupidity thwarted Michelangelo's dream
of carving the tomb for Pope Julius II from Monte
Borla marble. Michelangelo with two servants and
horses, as his friend Condivi explains, spent eight
months seeking the right vein of marble for the tomb,
was then forced—with his Genoese sailors and their

boat—to move south from Serraveza, from which the marble could have been loaded for transport to Ostia, up the Tiber to Rome. The tomb was never finished.

A ruder—say less elite—use of the chisel is afforded by architecture: the Maidens of the Erectheum and their replicas with arms (made before the originals were damaged) beside the lake at Hadrian's Villa; the fast-eroding, benignly smiling Father Tiber at the end of the lake, Romulus and Remus nestled in his lap; the stone alligator which plants itself without a peer for naturalness in a semi S on the lake coping across from the Maidens, his jaws with sawtooth teeth parted rapaciously—or in a smile? The verity of the alligator has a counterpart in the rather unsimilar gargoyle alligator heads protruding from the band of stone which extends above the gate of the King's castle at Sintra—the gate itself overhung by a lion head which frowns and one which smiles; the approach shrouded at the base by dense maidenhair fern despite the sun-baked farmland below. Lions, recurring under many a king, we have again in the row of five or six with open mouths before what was the palace at Delos; also in Italy's lion fountains and in St. Mark's lion on the column beside the quay bordering St. Mark's Square.

A use of the chisel, seemingly more utilitarian than portraiture, is Italian intarsia work depicting flowers, bees and butterflies—as in a notable table top in the castle drawing rooms at Montegufoni belonging to the Sitwell family; or as in the severely geometric olive, black and white intarsia screen setting apart the memorial chapel to Bishop Panteleone, founder of the church in Ravello. The pulpit is guarded by six bowlegged lions, each with a different face, three male, three female.

The stonecutter in Italy has brought to perfection the art of paving as seen in almost any Italian city: the concentric fan of street cobbles, the curbstone protruding in a half circle and mortised into the half eclipse of the adjoining one; not to mention the use of wall stones, protruding singly at intervals to form a stair such as reinforces the roadside wall up the nearly vertical hill road to Cortona; again in the 9- or 10-feet tall stone shutters still in use on the church at Torcello—each a single piece of stone and originally a protection against pirates.

The Knife | 27

This feeling for work with stone one sees in the floor mosaics from Herculaneum at the National Museum in Naples: black designs on white—a wall-of-Troy or interlinked eights enclosing separate symbols, the X, the axe, the box, the cross, the circle, the oval. A variant carried out in Greece in black and white pebbles constitutes a study in itself: the stair levels up the path to the citadel on Linos; the spray of heliotrope, black on white, gracing the approach to the door of a formal home on Santorini.

Stonework in Italy is matched by engineering—by the tunnel, straight or sometimes a half serpentine; by the expedient to combat erosion: the arrow of implanted stone on a precipitous hillside; by the sheared rock precipice on the road from Perugia to Rome, where gorge after gorge is intersected by lesser ravines clad with vines like the vertical vineyards of Ravello. Home and grapes are often guarded by a wrought-iron gate at the top of a flight of steps cut from the rock. Such triumphs of hand labor are miniature, however, compared with the thirteen years' labor by 300,000 slaves in rearing the Temple to Zeus at Olympia. Even works of hand by the best stonecutters, one finds dwarfed by spirit, as symbolized by the grassy mound memorializing the dead at Marathon, near the stele of the Athenian soldier associated in one's mind with Phedippedes who, too excited after fighting at Marathon to lay aside shield, sword and leg guards, ran the twenty-six and a half miles to Athens in an hour to announce as he fell exhausted, "We won."

In valor, there is small room for egotism. As Confucius says, "If there be a knife of resentment in the heart, the mind fails to act with precision."

SALT

ALDOUS HUXLEY

H̲ow do you catch birds?"

"By putting salt on their tails," the old gentleman from next door gravely replied.

"Salt? Just ordinary salt?"

"Just good old sodium chloride," he assured me.

Five minutes later, armed with a butterfly net and several ounces of salt in a small paper bag, I was out in the garden, on the prowl for birds. I stalked a thrush on the lawn, then two sparrows among the crocuses, then a pied wagtail. Long before I could get near them, they were gone. I changed my tactics and started to throw my salt by the handful at every bird within sight—at a chaffinch in the apple tree, at a blackbird, and finally at a fat domestic pigeon that fluttered down and was strutting along the garden path just ahead of me. Several grains landed on the pigeon—two or three of them, I distinctly saw, on his tail. "Got him!" I shouted triumphantly. Startled, the pigeon noisily flapped his wings and flew away. I burst into tears. That was before 1900, when Queen Victoria was still on the throne.

And here is another faded memory connected with sodium chloride—the memory of someone singing a music-hall ditty that was already ancient when I first heard it, sixty years ago. The face of the singer is a blank; but I can still hear the words—words that, to my well-brought-up little ears, seemed shockingly indelicate. "Kissing a man without a mustache is like eating an egg without salt." (From walrus and handlebar, one's mind wanders to those grand Victorian beards that covered such a multitude of physiognomic sins. How, one asks oneself, did the girls react to *those?* Kissing Karl Marx must have been like eating an egg with a sauce of Dead Sea brine.)

It was in 1902 that I heard that song. Thereafter,

for some time, salt was something I never thought about—just took for granted as the white stuff to which one helped oneself at meals. It re-emerged into the light of consciousness some eight years later during a summer holiday in Switzerland. We were eating our picnic lunch in a high meadow, bright with Alpine flowers and alive with butterflies and grasshoppers. The hotel had provided the usual hikers' lunch—bread, cheese, slices of cold veal, hard-boiled eggs and a good supply of salt. While we were eating, a browsing nanny goat approached, made a beeline for the tin plate onto which the salt had been poured and in a trice had licked up all the seasoning without which hard-boiled eggs are as insipid as mustacheless kisses. The incident aroused my curiosity. Why should goats be so passionately interested in sodium choloride? And, for that matter, why should people be so passionately interested? And what about those noble oriental characters in novels, who refrained from killing an enemy because he had once partaken of their salt? What about that strange verse in the Gospel: "Ye are the salt of the earth: but if

49777

the salt have lost his savour, wherewith shall it be salted? it is thenceforth good for nothing, but to be cast out, and to be trodden under foot of men."

Back at school I made inquiries of my pastors and masters; I consulted encyclopedias. In a short time I had learned quite a lot about salt in relation to physiology, to myth and history, to politics, social customs and religious symbolism.

The first thing I discovered was the reason for the odd behavior of that nanny goat in the Alpine meadow, and for the still odder behavior of the bison, antelopes and such like creatures that will travel hundreds of miles to get a taste of a saline spring or an efflorescence of sodium salts. It is because they are strict vegetarians that goats and the other salt-craving animals behave as they do. For all mammals, sodium salts are a vital necessity; they cannot live without them. But grass contains little of these indispensable substances. In regions of the world where the soil is especially poor in sodium compounds, grass-eating animals are subject to a physiological drive that sends them, from time to time, on compulsive pilgrimages to distant mineral springs and salt licks. They are like dope addicts, compelled by an irresistible inner need to find a Connection, a source of chemical supply.

And what of human beings? Primitive hunters and the nomads who live by pasturing herds of cattle and flocks of sheep and goats can get on very well without salt. The meat they eat, the blood that many of them drink, are rich in sodium chloride. It was only after the invention of agriculture, only after the hunters and drovers settled down, only when sodium-poor cereals rather than sodium-rich meat became the staff of life, that salt entered human history. Like exclusively vegetarian ruminants, predominantly vegetarian humans felt a need for extra sodium, a need that expressed itself in a compulsive craving for salt. Those who lived near the sea satisfied their craving by evaporating salt water; those who lived inland imported salt from the coast, or scraped up the contaminated sodium chloride which, here and there, covers the ground with a salty crust. (The Biblical salt that has "lost his savour" was probably this mixture of mud and sodium chloride.)

An inland source of sodium chloride was a treasure

worth fighting for. Tacitus, the Roman historian, tells us that during the reign of Nero, two German tribes, the Chatti and the Hermunduri, fought a great battle for the control of "a river that produced salt in plenty, and bounded their territories." The war was ideological as well as economic; for the combatants believed that salty places are "specially near to heaven, and that the prayers of men are nowhere more attentively listened to by the gods." These Teutonic barbarians were not alone in thinking that there was something supernatural about salt. Agriculture had made civilization possible, and civilized humanity's cereal diet had made of salt a vital necessity —given it, so to speak, a power of life and death. One prayed to heaven for good crops and, along with prayers and first-fruits, offered to the gods the precious salt, without which even the best crops would be inadequate.

"Salt, as the law testifies, is a substance specially dear to the gods." So wrote Plato. And his estimate of sodium chloride was shared by the rest of the ancient world. Like the Greeks and the Romans, the Hebrews offered up salt with their sacrifices and made

"Covenants of Salt" with one another over their sacrificial banquets. To break such a covenant, or to kill a man with whom one had eaten salt, was not merely a breach of human law; it was an act of cosmic disobedience, a sacrilegious affront to heaven.

Like the goat and the bison, cereal-eating man finds the taste of salt agreeable, and finds it agreeable because he has a physiological need for sodium chloride. But besides being a condiment and a constituent of blood plasma, salt is bactericidal and inhospitable, in high concentrations, to fungi. Until the invention of canning at the beginning of the nineteenth century, followed by the development of refrigeration in our own time, salting and drying were the only effective ways to preserve food from spoilage. Catholics had to eat fish on Fridays; and for practically everyone, until very recent years, the only available fish was salt fish. And the brine barrel was not exclusively reserved for fish. In earlier centuries, Europe knew nothing of maize or oil cake. Consequently there was never enough winter fodder. Only the indispensable minimum of animals could be kept alive through the cold weather. Around Michaelmas Day, September 29th, the rest were slaughtered and reduced to salt beef, salt pork and a huge variety of spiced and briny sausages. From October to April, fresh meat was almost unobtainable. And this lack of fresh meat was accompanied by an even completer lack of fresh vegetables. By the time spring came around again, most people were on the verge —and some were well over the verge—of scurvy and pellagra.

"Ye are the salt of the earth." The phrase refers, presumably, to both of the traditional uses of salt— to supplement a diet deficient in sodium chloride and give zest to insipid carbohydrates, and to preserve food that would otherwise be lost by decomposition. Those who are the salt of the earth perform the double function of giving meaning to human life and of preserving human societies from breaking down into moral and intellectual decay. The prophet who sells out to vested interests, the artist who goes commercial, the philosopher-seer who ignores his insights and conforms to the taboos of the tribe—in their different ways, these intrinsically salty people have lost their savor and their antiseptic qualities and are good for nothing but to be cast out.

After the burst of inquiry triggered by the episode of the Alpine goat, salt retreated once again from my field of consciousness. True, I was briefly amused, when I began to earn a little money, to discover that my meager salary took its name from the *salarium*, or allowance for the purchase of salt—one of the Roman legionary's fringe benefits.

A more serious renewal of my interest in salt came only much later, and was a by-product of my growing concern with the problems of population. There are now three thousand million members of the human species. By the year 2000, unless something very bad or unexpectedly good should happen in the interval, there will be six thousand millions. To maintain the miserable standard of living now current among a majority of the human race, the world's agricultural production will have to be doubled within the next forty years. If the present miserable standard is to rise, agricultural production will have to be multiplied by a factor of three or even four. How can it be increased to this extent? Among other ways, by irrigating hundreds of millions of acres of the world's deserts. Once again, how? Among other ways, by taking the salt out of sea water and of inland sources too briny to be usable.

Cheap atomic energy may make it feasible to desalinate and pump sufficient quantities of water to bring fertility to the dry places of the earth. But what will be done with all the extracted salt? One has visions of great mountains of sodium chloride—more than sufficient to put a pinch on the tail of every bird in the world, with enough left over to catch all the flying saucers and even perhaps (we sorely need them) a few million angels.

BREAD

RUMER GODDEN

"Crusty bread baked here." That, up to a year ago, was a sign in our village shop. "Crusty bread." Why was that so enticing? I think because it conjured up more than a vision—a delectable smell and taste. The bakery behind the shop was a warm and pleasant place, for us—if not for the baker, Mr. Morris, who had flour in his lungs and had to get up at half-past four in the morning to get his great brick oven hot; it was heated by fagots and logs. It was true he had an electric mixer, but he still cut and shaped the dough by hand, and the tins were still slid into the oven by him and brought out on a long-handled wooden peel. He was a faithful and tireless servant to his customers. His bread was delivered around the village by his own van and on Good Friday mornings the whole street was fragrant with the smell of spiced Hot Cross Buns, baked and delivered in time for our breakfasts. Mr. Morris' son, Joe Morris, iced all the birthday cakes in the district, and on Christmas Day processions of people brought their turkeys to be roasted in the bakery oven so that all the family could go to chapel or church.

Last year Mr. Morris died of his flour. Joe went to work for a large combine, and the shop now buys its bread from wholesale bakeries. But this is not a lament for the old days. We all know that nothing tastes as good as freshly baked bread; that connoisseurs will have nothing but flour milled with stone, water-cooled; that there is nothing that makes a home as homely as the smell of baking, or of dough set in a basin on the hearth to "prove." All this is old hat as my daughter would say. Most of us are not connoisseurs and we have not time to bake our bread; it would indeed be silly, except on special occasions, perhaps, with the variety offered us in the shops. I would even go further away from lament: In most places one used to be dependent on a single baker; if he was good, it was all very pleasant, but if he had "a poor hand with dough," as they said, or "no feeling for dough," one was doomed to heavy, soggy bread and no alternative. Nowadays, except in really remote villages, if anyone eats poor bread, it is his own fault.

There are always croakers. "Plastic in frogskin" was how someone described a modern factory-baked loaf. Yes, that is a graphic description if one insists on white flour, on even texture (which bread should not have), on no holes (when bread should be aerated) and, to save the trouble of cutting it, that the loaf should be sliced and wrapped. By then it has gone mechanically too far and is "dead."

Why do so many people insist on these things? Well, there has always been a certain snobbery about bread and once it was a mark of social position to eat fine white bread. Juvenal, who died in A.D. 140, wrote that for the entertainment of a noble guest "a delicate loaf was reserved, white as snow and kneaded of the finest flour." But now, of course, the snob who really knows eats stone-milled whole meal, or garlic or French bread—and, in a modern bakery, he will find these. An ordinary bakery, in an ordinary town or city, has white bread, brown bread, whole-meal bread, in such shapes as farmhouse, cottage, long tin, short tin, sandwich, twists. It has French, Vienna, Norwegian and Swedish bread—rolls, bâtons, rye bread, nut bread, malt bread, raisin bread, seed bread, garlic bread, milk bread, health bread. And none of it, as sometimes in the old days, can be short weight, be made of weevily flour, or have chalk added. In fact, it has vitamins added.

According to a modern report, bread and flour provide more energy, more protein, more iron and more of the two vitamins B^1 and Nicotinic acid than any other single food. In other words, in spite of all the warnings of the slimming diets, bread is good for us, and among basic foods, bread is the cheapest. In fact, it is a nutritional bargain. Even the ecstatic advertising on some of the wrapped bread—"Sun-blest," "Sun-kissed," "Golden Prairie"—is unexpectedly true, because corn will not ripen without sun:

Back of the loaf is the flour
and back of the flour is the mill
and back of the mill is the heat and the shower
and the sun and the Father's will.

Bread has always been more than itself. The word "bread," for instance, is a synonym for food—the word "crumb," for poverty or a pittance. "Bread and salt" in the East signifies the trust of hospitality: "He has eaten my bread and salt and I cannot harm him."

"Cast thy bread upon the waters," is a symbol of trusting generosity—not counting the cost—"for thou shalt find it after many days." Or, as one child succinctly put it: "It shall come back buttered."

Bread and water instantly calls up punishment, solitary confinement. Bread and butter sprinkled with sugar evokes the nursery and, for me, fairy tale princesses; bread and meat: the great castles of the Middle Ages; bread and wine: holiness, ritual life— "these creatures of bread and wine" as the Book of Common Prayer so beautifully calls them.

"Creatures" is not a misnomer. A few, very few foods have a quality of livingness: Vinegar, as well as yeast, has to have a "mother." We say of wine that it must breathe, mature. But bread seems even more alive. The dough has to be "proven." Just like us, it has to "rest"—to "work"—to "rise." Even the big factories, with all their speeded-up methods, have to recognize this. The staff of life has power, and it is a good power.

In poem, myth, proverb or parable, bread always signifies something desirable, good and wise: "Keep at three paces' distance any man who does not like bread, music or the laugh of a child." Or again, "If you have one loaf, sell half and buy a lily." Bread's very superstitions are linked with holiness. Here in Britain the first loaf made from the last sheaf of wheat reaped in a field is supposed to have protective powers. In some parts of England and Wales a professional "sin eater" used to come to a funeral and, for a fee, eat a loaf of bread by which he could take the dead person's sins on himself. That cryptic sentence of Ophelia's in *Hamlet*—"The owl was a baker's daughter"—comes from a legend that Jesus once went into a baker's shop to ask for a loaf of new bread. The baker's wife gave Him one but her mercenary daughter objected in an angry whisper to the size of it. She was promptly turned into the screech owl (which does not screech but hisses).

There are stories of the saints in which, over and over again, bread was made holy: St. Elizabeth of Hungary, when her husband the King found her carrying the forbidden bread to the poor and forced her to open her kirtle, found the bread changed to roses. Hot Cross Buns, according to the people of Assisi, we owe to St. Clare: on Good Friday, the Archbishop used to distribute small loaves to the poor. One year, he ordered the Saint to take his place. She was so modest that she was appalled but, under obedience, did as she was told and every loaf she touched immediately had a cross on it.

These overtones, if we can call them that—these elements of the supernatural—have been with bread all through history. It gives one a strange feeling to see, in the British Museum, loaves, real loaves, baked in Egypt in 2100 B.C. These loaves were a version of "death bread," but they still have life in them, for life was still in the wheat grain, found in the same tomb: it sprouted when it was put into the earth. Bread was used as currency in Egypt, wages were paid in it but it was always venerated. That heat should change a sticky mass of dough into a loaf seemed holy to the Egyptians, and they had a goddess of the oven—as the Romans had with Fornax whose picture hung over the ovens of Rome. Her festival was kept on June 9: on that day the bakeries stopped work, the ovens were decorated, and garlands were hung around the necks of the asses who spent the rest of the year tramping around and around to turn the mill. While the asses rested, the bakers had a feast.

Long before Roman times, the Greeks had identified bread with religion. They worshiped both grain and bread, and had their own goddess of the bread grains, Demeter, much more powerful than Fornax, being the sister of Zeus, the mother of Persephone and the Earth Mother. Every autumn there were ceremonies for her in Athens and at the bread temple at Eleusis. It was the Greeks who first made bread an integral part of religious ritual.

The Arabic word for bread means life, but east of Asia Minor, rice is usually held in more veneration (wheat being rare). The unleavened bread of Persia and India is more usually made of maize and is not the purest of food. Among the Chinese, I could not find a single reference to bread. Rice cake, hot cake, bean curd and noodles are in all the classics although not a word of bread. But then the Chinese, cultured and philosophical as they were, sages many of them, were not mystics.

It was with the Jews that the true mysticism of bread began. Its primitive form was "matzo"—a flat round biscuit, still eaten at the Passover. In the Jewish religion the ritual kept in the home is most important: on Friday evenings in Orthodox homes, candles are lit, two loaves (usually twist loaves covered with poppy seeds) are put on the table, a blessing— the sanctification of the fruits of the earth—is said over them and the bread is broken, a piece given to each person, who eats it with salt.

The Hebrew word for "manna" means "What is it?" The Bible tells us it was made of the "corn of heaven" and from St. Paul we learn that the Ark of the Covenant contained a pot of manna. What many of us forget is that when Christ at the Last Supper initiated the consecration of bread, this was not a new idea to the apostles: they were Jews and so they naturally associated bread, manna, with God.

Christ used bread in His teachings all through His ministry. It was in the miracle of the loaves and fishes and in the meal that He prepared for the disciples on the shore of Galilee after His Resurrection. He made Himself known to the disciples at Emmaus by the breaking of bread (the recusants adopted this as a sign to one another during the persecutions in England after the Reformation). He brought it into the prayer He taught as all sufficient—the Our Father: "Give us this day our daily bread," a sentence that, as the great St. Teresa of Avila wrote in *The Way of Perfection*, can be interpreted to mean simply our daily food or the reception of Christ Himself, "The Living Bread."

In the early days of the Christian church, people brought their own loaves to be consecrated. Nowadays, the altar bread in the Anglican/Episcopalian churches varies with the lowness and highness of that particular church. It can be household bread cut into dice—as is used in Nonconformist churches. Or it can be purest wheat wafers—although these, in the Church of England, are illegal, strictly speaking, having been so ruled twice by the Judicial Committee of the Privy Council. Why? Perhaps because wafers are Popish—they are always used by Roman Catholics. But whatever the bread, it must be pure wheat, just as church wine must be pure grape and church water unadulterated.

I think this insistence on the real thing, untainted, unalloyed, is a valuable reminder. These are fundamental things, we should not lose touch with them, and there is a danger of our doing that nowadays, especially those of us who live in cities. It is startling to think, for instance, that few of us, now, know the taste of pure water—our supply is so disinfected and sterilized. Wine has been ousted from the average home by beer or spirits. But we still have bread. As with all fundamental things we never get tired of it

—cottage loaf, farmhouse, rolls, baps, nurex, whole meal.

"The corn was orient and immortal wheat which never should be reaped nor was ever sown. I thought it had stood from everlasting to everlasting."

Ordinary bread. Crusty bread baked here.

GLASS

ALAN PRYCE-JONES

I t isn't a diamond, Daddy," says the child, "it's only glass." Only glass, indeed! I put down my drink, close the window, rub my spectacles, switch on a light, pick up a magnifier and examine the tiny object lying in an ashtray. Only glass, when everything I have been touching is glass, too. Glass that lets in light, or keeps it out, glass that ripples and bends, glass that plays tricks with the universe, cutting it down to dollhouse size, blowing it up gigantically, making jokes at its expense through the curve of a mirror. By comparison, who wants a diamond?

One day about fourteen thousand years ago, so Pliny tells us (though Pliny could not count as well as we), somebody made an open fire, in which sand and soda came together. Why they did so, we cannot now guess. It was not a cooking intention (certain dishes may still taste like sand and soda, but not by design). It was not an experiment. All this happened in Mesopotamia, some six thousand years before the same people, in another inventive flash, discovered the art of writing. There, however, unrecorded and unrecordable, on the sand lay a fragment of glass. And from that moment spring half the wonders of our civilization: the windows of Chartres Cathedral and a television tube, a Pyrex dish and our knowledge of the moon, both the indoor thermometer and the sunlit warmth which it records.

Glass is unlike anything else. The experts call it a physical condition rather than a thing. For thousands of years it was a magical kind of pottery: a green glaze on powdered quartz. No wonder the Egyptians used it as jewelry, mixing it with the precious stones which ornamented the living and the dead. For in those days the art of blowing glass had not been invented. Even now, it seems miraculous that glass can go so easily from one condition to another. Like a human quality, it is at one moment liquid, malleable, all possibility. The next, it has cooled into a rigid set of attitudes. There is something godlike about the role of the glass blower. Out of a shapeless bubble he is creating order and symmetry as if he were reliving the sixth day in the Garden of Eden. His work is one of the few things as brittle as himself.

It is another of the human aspects of glass that it affects whatever it touches. My drink is not at all the same if I drink it out of a teacup. My view is not the same if I open the window again. For glass is not merely a physical condition; it is also a personality. In spite of fires and air raids and urban improvements, there is still quite a lot of pre-Victorian glass in European city windows. Tinted slightly mauve, and fixed in small panes, it gives the world an aquatinted air. A London square, seen through such a window, looks as if it came from Mrs. Gaskell's *Cranford*—all street criers, and gossip and linkmen. Replace the panes with a great square of plate glass, and at once a European city looks not picturesque but old-fashioned. The window demands something spectacular to gaze upon, something like the lake front of Chicago or the view across the bay of San Francisco from the top of Nob Hill.

This is part of the mystical element in glass. Not for nothing did Christianity and clear glass come into the world together. For it was the existence of clear glass which made colored glass possible, and with it a whole new range of emotions. The great cathedrals of all epochs owe their majesty largely to their windows; and often, if I drink a colored liqueur, or watch the starry transformations of a kaleidoscope, I amuse myself by remembering that these trivial pleasures for the eye are no different from the splendors of Bourges or York: they are simply the play of light through a substance so generous that it allows equal access to every emotion, from purely sensuous pleasure to the raptures of the saints.

The hospitality of glass cannot be exaggerated. Indeed, without glass a great many sensuous pleasures would not exist for us. Where would colored drinks be without glass to contain them? I cannot imagine a marble urn of crème de menthe, or a porcelain claret bottle. Indeed, it is to the condition of glass that other containers aspire. We like our china paper-thin, so that the light streams through it; we prefer our urns of alabaster. But none of these materials react with such sparkle as glass to the exterior world. Not only does it allow the claret to glow through from within, but it steals light from the sun whenever it can. Give it a facet, or even a curve, and it will wink back at you with the manifold refraction of a prism.

Nothing about a house gives so keen a sense of hospitality. This is partly because glass is a gay substance. We speak, not without reason, of crystal laughter; and we link the glitter of a chandelier with comfortable-sounding objects like goblets and tumblers. The transparency helps. After all, we like seeing through our friends as well as catching a sudden reflection of their brightness. And so the presence of glasses in a room at once gives it a party air. They symbolize the impermanence, the headiness, of human contacts as well as their extreme breakability. Evelyn Waugh once described the noise of a sophomore party at Oxford as that of the British upper classes "baying for broken glass." But it isn't only sophomores who bay. Every partygoer recognizes a dangerous moment when the thread of pleasure is drawn so tight that it looks like snapping. Something has to go—and it probably won't be the unwanted guest. Grownups may regret at such moments that they are supposed to be too civilized to relieve their feelings by smashing something.

This emotion, however, is only the dark side of a surface essentially merry. Very few people dream of letting off steam by throwing Sèvres about, or tearing the marquetry to pieces. But most glass is neither Waterford nor Bristol; it is merely a brave and transitory show, quickly replaced. And so it preaches a kind of sermon to our subconscious. We feel reassured that we need not be serious all the time when we give ourselves to the moment just as easily as we pick up a glassful of good fellowship in its fragile container.

Mirrors? They play a very different part. Always at work, noticing, duplicating, enlarging, modifying, mirrors are the busiest of domestic objects. They can never refuse their services. Even if they are pointed upwards, they have a whole arc of the firmament scribbled over their faces. The smallest of them carry in their silver depths some echo of Versailles and Herrenchiemsee. They speak so much of kings and queens and treaties and state occasions that we forget all about their practical qualities, although we may think of a broken looking glass as the typical sign of seedy decay. All the same, it is those practical qualities which lead me toward a world in which I have no place. I see telescopes, spectroscopes, electron tubes and all the paraphernalia of science, down to the humble pipette. Glass seems to be everywhere. It captures sound, it augments heat, it helps to make light out of a vacuum, it pulls the stars out of the sky in order to give them the human qualities of a landscape.

Stop! I would rather think about the glass dress designed for the Infanta Eulalia of Spain somewhere in the 1890's. Unluckily it refused to fold. She must have looked like a Tiffany lampshade in action. Or I recall the glass flowers arranged with such perverse ingenuity in a museum at Harvard. Yet even when glass becomes eccentric, it seldom loses its intrinsic beauty. If one looks in the window of a junk shop, one will see the most extravagantly curious ornaments. The dreadful china ones look what they are: dreadful. But even the shrimp-pink glass cornucopias embossed with gilded rosettes, the opalescent lily shapes and the leaded panels for a front door with one wintry tulip in the center have kept some kind of contact with the original material out of which they were made—the hot liquid poured like honey in Bohemia or Italy.

Elinor Wylie once wrote a book called *The Venetian Glass Nephew*. That was nearly forty years ago, and at the time it looked as though her fancy were too exotic to be compelling. Now, however, in a world where, more and more, glass makes inroads into every activity among people whose expression has, more and more, become glazed by the pressures of living, some such transformation seems almost credible. I should never be surprised to find a crack in one finger or a chipped ear lobe. Scientists tell us that eventually the world will turn to ice as the poles creep together. And that will be the end of it: one immense, silent, empty crystal. A girandole in space.

GRASS

JOSEPH WOOD KRUTCH

O f all the green things which make up what Goethe called "the living garment of God," grass is one of the humblest, the most nearly omnipresent and the most stupidly taken for granted—a miracle so common that we no longer regard it as miraculous. To some (poor things), it is merely what you try to keep the dandelions out of, or what you strike a golf ball across. But even such as they are paying some tribute to it. To those of us a little more aware of the great mystery of which we are a part, its going and its coming, its flourishing and its withering are a sort of soft *ostinato* accompaniment in the great symphony of the seasons.

Even in the arid Southwest it springs up bravely for a few short weeks. In California the brown hills turn to emerald overnight. And in the gentler, more circumspect East one hardly knows when the great awakening takes place. So imperceptible but ineluctable is its progress that those of us who watch for it never quite catch the very moment when the transformation occurs. While our backs are turned, it is alive again, and no other phenomenon of spring is at once so quiet and so all enveloping. If there are astronomers on Mars peering at us as our astronomers are peering at their planet, they must see, much more dramatically, what we see there—a globe turning green. Martian vegetation is perhaps only a dry lichen like that we see clinging on bare rocks near the summits of our highest mountains, but ours is a green carpet, soft to the feet, restful to the eye, and announcing to all living things that spring is here again.

But what is this thing called grass? "Why," says the botanist, "that is a question easy to answer." Grass, properly so-called, is any one of the numerous genera and species which compose that family of monocotyledonous flowering plants long known as the Gramineae. Unfortunately, its early evolutionary history (like that of all the flowering plants) is obscure since the fossil record is scanty, but at least we can say with reasonable certainty that no grass carpeted the earth in that long ago when the first air-breathing animals crawled out of the water. Also that it was not until the cool weather of the Miocene (say a mere forty million or so years ago) that it became a dominant plant and thus made possible the flourishing of the herbivorous mammals over a more peaceful earth where the bellowing of the dinosaurs had given way to the lowing of herds. Then, only yesterday, as world history goes, grass conferred upon our own species that tremendous blessing called wheat.

For a less dusty question and answer we must turn to the poets, many of whom have had their say, although only Walt Whitman put grass at the center of a magnum opus:

A child said, What is the grass? fetching it
to me with full hands; . . .
I guess it must be the flag of my disposition,

out of hopeful green stuff woven.
Or I guess it is the handkerchief of the Lord,
A scented gift and remembrancer designedly
    dropt,
Bearing the owner's name someway in the corner,
    that we may see and remark, and say Whose?

Few today have time for Whitman's meditations
or for his quiet pleasures. Most of us are too desper-
ately busy seeking recreation, entertainment and
amusement to experience that Joy for which all the
other things are but disappointing substitutes—as
essentially ersatz as plastic for china, neon lights for
dawn and sunset, or the corner grocer's horror offered
us in place of that other great gift of grass called
bread.

"Joy be with you," people used to say when part-
ing from a friend. Now the modish farewell is, "Have
fun!" Sometimes those thus sped on their way actually
do have fun; often they do not; and even the most
successful in this enterprise are not too much to be
envied. Those of us who want something more than
fun, whether it be the exaltation of great art or the

mystical experience of "belonging" to something greater than one's self, are a little afraid of being called highbrows or "nature lovers" because neither grass nor Wordsworth's meanest flower that blows are what we call "fun things." They can be something much more rewarding, nevertheless.

Henry David Thoreau once explained that he did not drink wine because he was afraid it might "spoil his taste for water." Henry loved to shock by "going too far" in defending what he wanted to defend, and perhaps he was going too far when he said that. If ours were an age tending toward the puritanical and the ascetic, he might be a dangerous influence, persuading us to surrender in the name of simplicity things much worth having. But since our manners and our morals are not, whatever else they may be, puritanical or ascetic, his voice is more worth hearing than that of those who call for more complexity, for madder music and for stronger wine. All of these pay diminishing returns.

We boast that this is the age of abundance, and the proudest achievement of our best intentioned men is that, for the first time in history, abundance has been democratized or, to put it somewhat sourly, that now as never before nearly everybody can have rather too much of many things not worth having. Deprivation can kill joy, but so, almost as certainly, can superfluity, for though we always want more, the limiting factor is ultimately what we can take in. More toys than he can play with are a burden not a blessing to any child be he five or fifty. It is disastrous to own more of anything than you can possess, and it is one of the most fundamental laws of human nature that our power actually to possess is limited.

In 1689 Louis XIV ordered the following for his garden at Versailles: 87,000 tulips, 800 tuberoses, 400 lilies and 83,000 narcissus. In this egalitarian age there are not very many individuals likely to be able to be quite that absurd. But there are many who can and do make the same mistake for the same reason. You just can't take in or possess that many tulips, and if you are foolish enough to try, you will miss the violet by the mossy stone, and even more surely the "thought too deep for tears" which one violet or one tulip might inspire.

The happiness of the great, said Francis Bacon, consists only in thinking how happy others must suppose them to be.

In Bacon's time the term "status," so beloved of present-day sociologists, had not yet been invented, but Bacon had grasped the concept behind it. The desire for status is the same desire to be envied that Bacon had in mind, and being envied was what Louis XIV also was aiming at. "It will be evident to all," so he must have said to himself, "that no one else in all the world can have as many tulips as I can, and they will envy me—though, God knows, the whole 87,000 of them look dull enough to me."

When grass becomes merely "a lawn," it is in danger of becoming what that sour economic puritan Thorstein Veblen said it always was, namely, a "status symbol," a display of conspicuous expenditure meant to demonstrate that its owner can afford to waste in mere display what might be used to produce wheat or vegetables. Veblen was wrong, because a lawn can also demonstrate a great truth which economists are prone to forget, namely, that beauty may be its own excuse for being. But a lawn can be what he called it, and there is no greater paradox than this transformation of the humblest and most unshowy of green things into a status symbol. Of course, neither your lawn nor mine (when I lived in Connecticut I had one) is that. But just to be sure that it isn't, a salutary experience can be had if we ask ourselves from time to time what our real reason for having a lawn is.

If we have any doubts, an experiment might be worth while. Lie down upon your lawn to see what happens. And while I would not advise that all lawns be surrendered to dandelions, I would suggest that you ask yourself, when one of those gay little miracles raises its flower toward the sun, whether you reach for the weed killer without first remembering Whitman's tribute:

Simple and fresh and fair from winter's close
    emerging,
As if no artifice of fashion, business, politics, had
    ever been,

Forth from its sunny nook of shelter'd grass—
  innocent, golden, calm as the dawn,
The spring's first dandelion shows its trustful
  face.

"All flesh is grass." For once the apostle and the scientist seem to be in agreement although they are not saying the same thing. To St. Peter all flesh is grass because man, too, "withereth and the flower thereof falleth away." To the biologist all flesh is grass in a more literal sense. No animal, man included, could exist if it were not for the fact that green plants mediate between him and the inanimate materials of the earth. They alone have the power of raising by one step the relative simplicity of the mineral to the complexity of the proteins indispensable to him. Where they leave off, his mysterious metabolism takes over. What was mineral but became protein now becomes that even more mysterious thing called protoplasm. And protoplasm is the base of all man's life, thought, imagination and ideals.

When after a time he also withers and the flower

thereof falls away, protoplasm descends the scale again to the merely mineral, and grass picks it up once more to repeat the cycle. The process began some billions of years ago and must continue as long as life lasts.

Which of the two truths is the most profound and the most important? The moral truth of the apostle, or the strange inhuman truth of the biologist? One is as old as civilization, the other almost as new as yesterday. And perhaps just because it is uniquely ours we tend to value it most highly. But we may be wrong. Many civilizations, some of them glorious, were created and then destroyed by men who were innocent of chemistry. But even those civilizations could not have been what they were had they not known what Peter and what Whitman knew. It is just possible that our civilization will fail because we do know one kind of truth and, in our pride, forget the other.

And now it seems to me the beautiful uncut hair of graves. . . .

It may be you transpire from the breasts of
    young men,
It may be if I had known them I would have
    loved them,
It may be you are from old people, or from off-
    spring taken soon out of their mothers' laps,
And here you are the mothers' laps.

This grass is very dark to be from the white heads
    of old mothers,
Darker than the colorless beards of old men,
Dark to come from under the faint red roofs of
    mouths.

THE COAT HANGER

AUBREY MENEN

A quarter of a century ago I decided that I would be an author. When I took that step, I knew quite well that when I reached fifty, I would be vain, conceited and greedy for money. That would be my character: I had made the acquaintance of several authors in their fifties and that was *their* character, so there was little chance that I would escape. It was a professional risk. The faces of actors at thirty or so begin to grow weather-beaten with public exposure; the character of an author is eroded, but more slowly, from the same cause: his personality is always on show.

Well, I am fifty. I have taken stock. It is all much

as I expected. I am vain. I talk incessantly about myself (I am doing so now). I am never satisfied with the praise that comes my way, and I never feel I have enough money. All this is right and proper for a writer of my age. I do not hold it against myself. What is quite wrong—what is shaming—is that I have too many clothes. I counted my coat hangers on my fiftieth birthday. What with suits, jackets and other items, there are sixteen of them. They are a monument to my moral cowardice. I would hide the story of why this is so except that at fifty one thinks continually upon the young: the description of my backsliding may serve as a warning.

The first thing a young writer must do is to make up his mind why he wants to write. Most young men write books to impress women and get themselves a rich wife—this, at least, is the belief of all the publishers I have known. I rejected this course. A rich wife would have been useful, but I observed that she would probably be an unhappy one. Being married to an author is certainly an honorable state, especially when he becomes a success. But then it is like being married to an Archbishop of Canterbury. Privately, he might lovingly admit that he would not be where he is had his wife not been constantly by his side: but she must on no account take this as an invitation to officiate at Evensong. She must remain in the back-ground, and so must wives of authors.

I might have decided to write for money. I rejected this, too. Writing for money nowadays means writing best sellers. To do that takes a mastery of the arts of verbiage, self-deception and calculated mendacity so great that it would carry a man to the highest political office in the land. I decided that if I had these gifts, they ought to be put to better use and, in any case, I hadn't got them.

I then thought of writing to express ideas that would make life a nobler and more beautiful thing, but I soon found I hadn't got these either. In the meantime, I had filled two large folio notebooks. One day I reread them. When I had finished, it struck me that I could not write at all.

A ghost came back from the past. It was of my old schoolmaster, Mr. Wilkinson, who had once violently crossed out every page of an essay of mine. He had selected one phrase that had particularly offended him and he had encircled it with violet ink. I had written "a veritable Pegasus." In the margin, he had written: "*What you mean is a HORSE.*" The incident remained in my mind because the very next day he committed suicide. We were never told at school why he had done it, but I could not help feeling at the time that it might have been because of my prose style. Now, reading my folio notebooks, I was sure it was.

I therefore sat down, day after day and month after month, to try to express clear thoughts in a plain way. This is very difficult to do in English. The Englishman does not like expressing clear thoughts in a clear style because it makes him feel French. Most English writers, therefore, do not try to do it. There are exceptions. David Hume was one, but he was a Scotsman who was driven to live in Paris to find anyone who would read his books. Still, Hume had proved that the thing could be done, and this encouraged me.

The results of my first few months of trying was a novel. It was a satire on British Colonialism, written as clear as clear could be. It was published in England and warmly welcomed as a graceful tribute from a young Indian to the sterling qualities of British Civil Servants under the Raj. Shaken by this, I sent the book to America. There, after some hesitation, the public saw what I meant, and I was launched as a writer.

But a peculiar sort of writer. I was not driven to give my thoughts to the world. On the contrary, I spent every morning sitting in my room, trying to find out what the devil my thoughts really were. I was not moved by the beauty and majesty of words. I spent every morning trying to write simple sentences as perfect as "the cat sat on the mat." In fact, somebody had given me a dog, who used to sit on the mat underneath my writing table. As an opening exercise for my evening's work, I used to write a few lines of her autobiography, as it might be told by herself. She had a simple outlook on life, so the autobiography began: "I was born in the house of a rich American," but neither she nor I got beyond the first chapter.

The task I had set myself was all-absorbing. I saw that if I were ever to complete it—to make, that is, a style of my own—I would have time for nothing else. I was an explorer, seeking treasure in the lush jungle of current English. I had to travel light, and in chosen company. I made up my mind to stay in my room as long as I could, to have no social life, and only one or two friends. I selected the rich American who had the house where the dog was born, and I had one suit made in which to go to see him. For the rest, I limited my wardrobe to slacks and shirts and sandals (for I was living on the Mediterranean) with one pullover for winter. That stopped me going out to parties. That is, it stopped me talking about literature until I knew how to write it—and it saved money which I would otherwise have had to earn by writing drivel and bombast. In my wardrobe, then, was only one coat hanger and I was very, very proud of the fact.

So I wrote, and the time passed. I was published. More time passed, and I was understood. I was happy; the dog waxed fat; the American was hospitable, but not pressing; and I still had only one coat hanger. But then I was overcome by a great desire to see my fellow writers and hear, face to face, what they thought of my work. So I packed my shirts and socks and pullover in a suitcase, borrowed an overcoat from a friend, put on my suit and bought a cheap rail ticket for London. The dog did not want me to go and, instead of sitting on the mat, sat on my suitcase. But like a perfect fool, I ignored her advice and went.

I arrived in London and a friend whom I had known in Italy took me to a literary party. It was a most distinguished one. I was very pleased. I should perhaps explain that literary life in London is a very compact affair. It is run on a principle of reciprocation, or, in other words, taking in one another's washing. Any dirty linen in the basket will probably be washed in public, but that cannot be helped. The vital thing is to be accepted into the laundrymen's union, so to speak. From the writers I saw around me, I felt I was well on my way.

In spite of the fact that I was a stranger, many of them spoke to me—not, indeed, about my books but about theirs, which was very kind of them, because it saved me from saying the wrong things: indeed, from saying anything at all. It was all most agreeable.

Then came the moment that, with natural vanity, I had been waiting for. Behind me, I heard a famous critic say, "Who is he?"

I heard the voice of my friend telling him.

"Ah," said the famous man. "I've seen his name. Is he any good?"

I held my breath.

"Yes," said my friend.

"Ah," said the famous man. "How's he doing?"

"He's working on a . . ."

"I mean," said the critic, testily, "is he making any money?"

My friend paused. Then, in a sage voice, he said, "Ah. Well, now. He's only had one suit in three years and . . ."

"Oh," said the great man. "Ah," he said, then, "*Well.*" In those three syllables, it was clear, I was summed up, damned and dismissed.

Some time after that, Rebecca West, noticing my disconsolate look, struck up a conversation with me.

We talked of H. G. Wells. She must have wondered why I asked how many suits he had. She answered, however. I forget the number, but it was a lot.

I returned to the shores of the Mediterranean, and my writing table. Once more the dog sat on the mat underneath it. I swore to her that never, never would I own more than one coat hanger and one suit, no matter how much money I made. She believed me. But then, she believed anything I said.

Well, I made some money, and for a while I kept my word. But somebody invited me to be best man at a wedding and I bought a suit for it, not to offend him. He christened his child with my first name, so I bought another new suit for the baptism, to bring luck to my godchild. I traveled. I moved to Rome. The dog came with me and still sat under my desk, but on a rug from Kairouan.

I went to receptions but, firmly, only those given to do honor to famous men of my profession. A considerable number passed through Rome. The years passed. The dog grew old and blind, and I grew careless of my resolves. I even went to a fashionable tailor.

Here I was surrounded by three master tailors and a special assistant was called whose only duty was to kneel in front of me and help me take off my trousers.

There were many fittings, and once when he did this, I noticed with acute embarrassment that, in a moment of abstraction, I had forgotten to put on my shorts. I apologized. I lied. I said that as I was dressing I had suddenly heard of the news of the death of Albert Camus. He had, indeed, died the night before, but I had never cared a jot for his works. The assembled tailors listened. Then the chief tailor said, in the tone of a priest giving absolution, "It does not matter at all. Mr. Mel Ferrer was here before you. He never wears shorts."

So it was all right. I had no need for Camus. Mr. Ferrer had preceded me. Effortlessly, as though to the manner born, I had adopted the habits of the *élite* of the world.

The suit was beautiful. It led to invitations from wearers of equally beautiful suits. Nobody asked any more how I was doing, because it was clear that I was doing all right. In the eyes of the world I had arrived.

Then one day, last summer, the dog who had been born in the house of the rich American retired to a corner of the house of a man with sixteen coat hangers and died. I buried her at midnight: my dog—and much else that I shall always miss.

THE SPOON

SANTHA RAMA RAU

Not long ago my young son and I were in India visiting my family and reacquainting him with the Indian half of his heritage (the other half is American). While we were there, in consideration of the more orthodox members of his Indian family—great aunts, second cousins and all of the relatives that Indians consider close kin—I had to instruct him in the etiquette and technique of eating a meal properly with his fingers. It isn't simple.

First he had to learn to be served and not to behave in the way that we do in our American home where we expect him to serve himself. The servant with the large ladle or cooking spoon comes to each member of the family and places rice on the large, round silver trays we call *thalis*. Then, into the small silver bowls, or *cutoris*, the servant spoons various kinds of curries, vegetables, yoghurt, pickles, lentils. Once served, my son had to learn to eat only with his right hand, never to touch food with his left hand, to use his fingers in such a way that they do not get dirtied beyond the first knuckle, to be sure to begin eating before his hostess because this is expected of any man or boy, and to master the countless other details of correct behavior at a formal Indian meal. By the end of our stay in India, my son was quite adept in the complexities of the Indian eating ritual.

When our Bombay visit ended, we went to London for a few days as a break in the long trip back to New York. There my son was invited to a children's tea party. The British, as everyone knows, make quite a performance out of the ceremony of High Tea—everyone, that is, except my son on that occasion. I will never forget his look of bafflement when he sat down at the tea table and faced a formidable array of food *and* of spoons. Which spoon went with which of the many delicious dishes? There were, of course, teaspoons to stir the very milky tea in the children's cups, then there were the spade-shaped spoons that the English like to use for ice cream, dessert spoons for the various jellies and trifles, large serving spoons next to each bowl of goodies, but, just to confuse matters in my child's mind, he found that he could eat the sandwiches and the cake with his fingers.

In America there was further instruction in this small area of living waiting for him. His father, an inveterate iced-tea drinker, introduced him to the long-handled spoons used for the cold drinks that are served in tall glasses. He also learned to recognize the wooden spoon I use in making cream sauces, the perforated spoon I use for scooping vegetables out of boiling water, the big mixing spoon, the tiny salt spoon that I still prefer to use on the table instead of the more popular (in America) salt shaker. Altogether, I could see, it really was an embarrassment of spoons.

But then I began to think about how pervasive and how basic this simple household item is and why it appears in so many different forms. It occurred to me that any woman who does her own housekeeping uses, in the course of a day, innumerable spoons. First, the spoon to measure early morning coffee (instant or regular), then the sugar spoon, the spoons to be set out for breakfast, the spoons to stir the coffee and eat the cereal, the cooking spoons for boiled, poached or scrambled eggs. Spoons all morning if you are a habitual coffee or tea drinker. The simplest soup-and-sandwich lunch requires a spoon, and the cooking of any kind of dinner involves spoons ranging from the ladle to the miniature spoon you use for measuring spices.

A friend of mine, an industrial designer, once told me that one of the first assignments her class in training school was given was to think up an implement that would serve *all* the purposes of eating a complete dinner, something that would combine the functions of the knife, fork and spoon. Most of the class, she said, finally settled for chopsticks because meat and vegetables can always be cut up in the kitchen, as they are in Chinese or Japanese cuisine, and consequently virtually anything can be eaten with chopsticks. Anything except soup. None of the students could think of a substitute for a spoon. Even in China and Japan, where long metal chopsticks are the main cooking implements, there is no way of serving most of the cooked food except with a spoon, and though knives and forks never appear on the table, soup spoons at a formal dinner are essential.

In Indonesia, in Ceylon, in the most obscure African village, people will fasten the scraped-out half-shell of a coconut to a stick to make, once again, that necessary implement—a spoon—to scoop water out of a brook for drinking, to use in the kitchen, to use as a measure in buying at the market or judging a recipe. A primitive variation, certainly, but don't we, in effect, do the same? After all, a "spoonful" is a standard measurement appearing in recipes the world over.

In a way, this taken-for-granted household implement carries its own important psychological significance. Thinking about it, I was rather surprised to find how evocative a spoon is of our earliest associations. It is, for instance, the first feeding instrument that a child knows after he is weaned from the breast or bottle. By now, in these psychology-conscious times, all of us have learned, one way or another, of the expression of love implicit in the offering of food to a child. The hand with the spoon in it, giving sustenance and satisfaction to the baby, will inevitably be a symbol of security, cherishing and consequently love. Indeed, this is only one part of a long tradition—a tradition that possibly has grown out of the early needs and dependencies of children on the people that feed them.

In virtually any country in the world, eating is a kind of ritual with its own rules, sometimes rather bizarre rules. Whether it is the Masai tribe of nomads in Kenya who will ceremoniously offer you fresh cow's blood sipped through a reed inserted in the vein of a living cow, or whether you are courteously handed the special delicacy of a fish eye in Japan, or whether you are surfeited with caviar and vodka by a Russian host, the principle is still the same. Food and the serving of it is a fundamental part of hospitality, a gesture from one human being to another of generosity, friendship and finally—to put it pretentiously —the brotherhood of man. If you can offer the first and basic need of mankind, food, to another person, you are to some extent expressing your wish for his good, for his survival, for his camaraderie, as well as your acknowledgment that both you and your guest share in "the human predicament," as the great English novelist, E. M. Forster, has called it.

If the most casual stranger walks into an Indian house, the owner, by the traditions of our society, must offer him something to eat and drink. In fact, an Indian friend of mine has, as her recurring nightmare, the dream of twenty-five people dropping in unexpectedly to dinner—and there is no food in the house! She always wakes consumed with guilt after this dream. How, she asks herself when she is still half asleep, could I not have seen to it that there was enough food for even the most unplanned number of visitors? There is so great a feeling about hospitality in India that there is even one day a year set aside for the worship and appreciation of household utensils. These, after all, are the objects that not only help to keep us alive, but also make it possible to show cordiality to other people. No wonder, then, that entertaining anywhere in the world usually involves the serving of food and drink, and that the objects that make this possible deserve individual attention.

In the West as much as in Asia, the classic present to a bride is the silver and cooking utensils she will need. Out of this basic sense of necessity combined with the higher sense of social grace grew the practice of creating ordinary household objects that are works of art. From the need to include elegance and beauty in daily living, great masters like Cellini fashioned with equal brilliance a statue as impressive and on as grand a scale as the Perseus and Medusa in the Loggia dei Lanzi in Florence, or small silver saltcellars for a dining table with their exquisite matching spoons. An artist like Jacques Rottiers put so much imagination and work into designing a 168-piece Louis XV silver dinner service that it recently sold for $579,600 at Sotheby's in London. Or think of the silversmiths of Queen Anne's period in England who labored to put the greatest artistry into the making of everyday table cutlery. They, too, knew the importance of delighting the eye with the most mundane utensils of our daily lives.

Even now, a sense of the value of both design and utility continues equally in the minds of housewives and manufacturers of household equipment. How stylishly the modern table silver is modeled, how sleek even the cheapest sets of stainless steel knives, forks and spoons appear, how well constructed for line and usefulness are the cooking spoons you can buy in any dime store. It is hardly surprising that so many kitchens these days are decorated—and I do mean *decorated*—with hook boards on which the cooking spoons hang proudly on display. This is partly for convenience of access, yes, but the sight of them is also esthetically pleasing. In the end the purpose of all the designers, from the most eminent artist to the anonymous draftsman, is the same: to bring grace and beauty into the home. And, as a result, the housewife's most monotonous tasks become that much more enriching.

Sometimes, through history to the present day, the whole ritual of eating and drinking takes on a religious aspect as well. This is very understandable when you remember the form of the communion service in a Christian church, or the traditional offerings of food from the worshipers to the gods in a Hindu temple, and the token handful of rice or fruit that a Brahman priest gives in blessing to attendants of a temple festival. It seems natural, then, in the West, that a logical decoration for the handles of spoons would be representations of religious figures, and in fact there are those charming sets of a dozen spoons known as "Apostle Spoons," each bearing the picture of a different apostle. In India the connection is somewhat different; still, it exists. After the religious ceremony of her marriage, a girl may take from her own family kitchen only the mortar and pestle for grinding spices, the silver pitcher for measuring milk and a cooking spoon. These make it possible for her both to set up her own kitchen and to have the means to prepare offerings for the gods.

The dignity of religion, the charm of beautiful workmanship, the earthy reality of the mechanics of living are all things that we become aware of as children. The instruments we use for cooking, serving or eating food have associations far beyond their simple utility. They are, for example, an intimate part of our feeling of hospitality—any hostess would bring out her best silver to honor special guests. And what is hospitality? Essentially a giving and receiving between people, a gesture of graciousness, the acknowledgment that the courteous offering of the fundamental necessities of life to another person distinguishes the civilized human being from the suspicious boor.

My son said to me the other day (in the incurable and only occasionally comprehensible jargon of small boys), "Hey, Mom, Billy and Peter are coming for supper. Neat, isn't it?"

"Neat" is exactly what I knew it wouldn't be if the three of them got together at table. However, with motherly self-restraint, I asked only what they would like to eat.

"Nothing creepy, O.K.? Like, I mean, no kind of liver or anything."

"Well, what?" (I've long since given up on liver anyway.)

"Something real cool, O.K.?"

"You mean cold cuts?"

"Oh, Mom, don't be such a spaz. I mean, like soup, maybe, and hamburgers and ice cream and like that. O.K.?"

It was certainly O.K. with me, and I started setting the table with the appropriate dishes and spoons and spoons and spoons. Hamburgers, like sandwiches, should be eaten with the fingers: a wonderful convention, since then there are no forks to wash. But I washed an amazing number of spoons that day.

WATER

ELIZABETH JANEWAY

Water is a universal symbol. Tamed and trickling out of the tap, softened and fluoridated, warmed in the boiler by fires burning million-year-old oil, it is still not quite a commodity. Even for city dwellers some dim memory stirs from time to time of those ancient eons when water or the lack of it ruled everything—the sites of habitation, the paths through the wilderness, the limits of hunting grounds, famine and abundance, life and death. It can still shatter human hopes and plans. Thirty years ago, the top soil in the plains states rose into the sky and blew away. Men had ploughed grazing land, counting on rain to bind the soil where the tough grass roots had been cut, and the rain did not come. A migration as great as that of the Mongols poured out of the Dust Bowl toward California. Steinbeck, in *The Grapes of Wrath*, recorded what happened to one bit of flotsam on one stream of this Diaspora. Today, I read in the papers, the Russians are ploughing the virgin Siberian lands as, in the last century, we ploughed the Dakotas. But the stubborn old gods of rivers and rains have not yet submitted to Marxist-Leninist discipline. Disappointing harvests are reported.

Water. "It has caused more wars in the Middle East," writes Freya Stark in one of her brilliant travel books, "than even religion." In the Middle East, that is quite a feat. But there are historians who trace the breakdown of the ancient civilizations along the Tigris, the Euphrates and the Indus to wars and raiding parties which breached dams and ruined irrigation and drainage systems. Whether the cities fell first and the aqueducts and irrigation ditches silted up through neglect, or whether they were deliberately destroyed to strangle the cities, they have never been rebuilt. Let us not imagine, in our smug pride of modernity, that engineers have yet become more powerful than statesmen, for even today, there is desert where once there was fertile land. Civilization takes water for granted, but that is civilization's mistake.

It's not a mistake, though, that will ever be made by those who live past the limits of "city water." Amidst all the denouncing of suburbia, let us give it credit for this: suburban dwellers must face some of the old facts of life, of living and of weather. In the country, water comes out of a well—save for that blessed, lucky trickle which flows to a favored few from a gravity-fed spring (and that is a trickle which, in August, may dwindle disastrously). Civilization, of course, has changed the Old Oaken Bucket into an electric motor pumping so many gallons a minute to a cistern from an artesian well, but it has not changed the nature of the emotions that go with procuring this water, only bunched them together into patches of intensity with stretches of complacence in between. But when the power goes out in a storm, so does the water supply.

Where we used to live, seventy miles from New York, the power had a habit of failing before the telephone lines went. Why this should be, I don't know. But the prudence of the telephone company in locating its poles and stringing its wires allowed messages to get through from neighbor to neighbor before the telephone lines went down and silence followed darkness. Thus, a spreading rash of calls would ripple out from the center of casualty: "We've lost our power. If you still have yours, fill the bathtubs quick." Then the householder (or his wife, if he was a commuter who spent his days in an ivory tower in the city) would go into action and fill tubs and buckets and pots and pans against the drought to come. After one ice storm, the water famine lasted for a week in some parts of the township, and luckier folk invited their neighbors in for baths.

From time to time, as families grew in size or new houses went up with their demanding machines for washing clothes and dishes, new wells had to be dug. Then the drillers would come with their rig and thump away at the ancient granite beneath our green countryside, and the owners would groan and shake a little, too, at the dollars that each hour of thumping represented. There was water, the drillers would report encouragingly, but not yet quite enough, three gallons a minute, five gallons a minute—would they never find the level that would deliver the necessary eight gallons a minute? On and on they went, like persevering, unsuccessful disciples of Moses, smiting the rock. Once a friend of ours, in despair after weeks of fruitless pounding, called in a water dowser. Our friend is the founder of one of the oldest and most respected public opinion polls. It seemed quaintly appropriate to think of an old man with a hazel twig in his hands questioning every foot of the poll taker's land on its water content. At last he said, "Dig here," and they dug, and found water. Of course, it was simply luck—whatever that means.

Water. It is a universal symbol, I wrote, but a symbol of what? Of birth and beginnings, as the scientists, the first chapter of Genesis and Dr. Freud all tell us? Life began in the sea, say the biochemists, when lightning discharges awoke, in the thin soup of almost-life, some monstrous protein molecules which married each other: this is our most modern mythology. An older story tells us that the Spirit of God moved on the face of the waters even before His command created Light: which might, after all, be simply a more majestic way of describing the same event. As for Freud, when he had rummaged through enough people's heads and stitched thousands of fragments of dreams together, he came to the cautious conclusion that "to dream of being in water or passing through a stream often symbolized the act of birth." Which is a nice, pedantic, and quite useless conclusion, for it leaves us with another set of waters unexplained. What shall we make of "the bitter, salt, estranging sea," or the rivers of Styx and of Lethe, which are the rivers of death?

We must think again. Water can symbolize birth, as it can symbolize death, but essentially its meaning is greater and simpler, and includes both. At the deepest level, water stands as the symbol of Change. Indeed, when St. John, in the Revelations, wished to describe the eternal landscape that would follow upon the Day of Judgment, he said, "There was no more sea." Changeless eternity could go no further.

Water is the present tense. It flows. It will not take a shape of its own, but will fill indifferently any jug or pitcher or cup, and then flow out and on, indifferent still, forgetful and uninfluenced. Its strength is the strength of movement. Even "still waters" must "run deep." If they do not, we distrust them and have made a pejorative word for such unnatural behavior —"stagnant," or standing. In New Mexico, the Indians believe that water can die. Mary Austin records the legend:

> At midnight drink no water
> For I have heard said
> That on the stroke of midnight
> All water goes dead.

Water is always now. It demands the present participle for its description—gushing, flowing, pouring, sprinkling. As every gardener knows, last week's soaking and next week's rain might as well not exist, unless we manage to string them together by constructing tanks and cisterns and reservoirs. Thirst is immediate. Water cannot be an event, it must be a presence. To make it so must be a primary concern of any stable society, great or small.

Modern man is astonishingly modest about his

achievements. I am not at all sure that this is a healthy state of mind. Might we not be more confident of our ability to deal with our future problems if we took a bit more pride in our successful solutions to problems of the past? Modesty is all very well for individuals, but civic pride can give a community a sense of wholeness and of its obligations to its citizens. We have somehow lost the knack of celebrating deeds of greatness today, and are apt to go off to the beach on the Fourth of July, each family by itself, instead of taking a little time to remember our heroes and refresh our pride.

I would like to see more holidays, and as one of them I would like to propose a Festival of the Waters. It might well be held on St. Swithin's Day. I imagine pilgrimages to the Tennessee Valley, to Grand Coulee and to Boulder Dam. I think of holiday tours along the St. Lawrence Seaway, with river steamers full of bands and picnickers toasting all that good sense, engineering training and peace between nations have wrought there. The irrigated valleys of California could show off their wealth.

Above all, each city should offer thanks to its sanitary engineers, who might appear with an accompanying guard of master plumbers—for even the grimmest nature may sweeten a little once it feels itself appreciated. The Mayor might read out the proud statistics citing the number of years since typhoid or cholera claimed a victim within his purlieus; and if the statistics should by any chance not be so proud, how quick the Mayor and the Department of Sanitation would be to improve them! And each year the ceremony would be crowned by the dedication of some new Wonder of Water: a handsome public pool, or a fountain with a bit of green about it, shining and leaping in the center of the city where passers-by could refresh their eyes. Or a boat basin. Or a new wing on the aquarium. Or—

But you see what I mean. Water is a universal symbol because it is a universal need. As we live now, it is beyond the power of the individual, in the vast majority of cases, to satisfy this need on his own. Only men working together can build reservoirs and aqueducts and dams and hydroelectric stations and sewage conversion plants and, soon no doubt, great structures to desalt the sea and make the desert blossom like the corn tassel and the alfalfa.

Our Festival of Waters, then, would be a holiday to celebrate the things that men working together can achieve. What could be more appropriate? For as we all know, the just and the unjust both get wet when it rains and thirsty when it does not. Too often, in the past, the just and the unjust have preferred to disagree and to create deserts rather than settle down and share out their water rights. But now our engineering knowledge is growing with the world's population, and with its need for water. Might not, for once, new skills combine with new needs? Might not the just and the unjust decide to work together, literally for dear life? And might not these projects to control the fluid strength and the eternal changeability of water teach us something about controlling the fluid strength and eternal changeability of human nature?

THE STOVE

RHYS DAVIES

The other day, when I was shown the resplendent microwave oven ("a meal turned out in a few minutes") that a well-off friend bought for his understandably pampered bride, I remembered a farmhouse stove of my childhood. Grandiose in a very different way, it was of nineteenth-century vintage and belonged to a husband-loving aunt of mine. She always refused to get rid of the handsome monster. In pleasurable accord with its mysteries, she was never daunted by its huge coal fire, cumbersome oven, complicated flues, hobs, trivets, griddle piece, pulley chains and jack for open roasting, fender, coal scuttle, pokers and ash raker.

She treated this stove, which lay in a chapel-like alcove of the enormous kitchen, with a diplomatic respect and wheedling devotion often given to the Author of our being. And well she might. The oven's massive iron door had an inset panel on which was carved, in the center of a design of wheat sheaves, a bearded figure of God on a throne, hand benignly raised in blessing. Every morning she black-leaded the entire main body of the stove, beginning by giving God's nose a generous dab, then, singing, burnishing the whole to a silvery black luster. It was like a matinal offering.

Her products from the revered stove were wonderful. I would be allowed to tear away the warm golden crusts overhanging her tins of bread, and it was of them I thought when, years later, I copied down a churchyard epitaph for a village baker:

Like to a Baker's oven is the grave
Wherein the bodies of the faithful have
A setting in: and where they do remain
In hopes to rise, and to be drawn again:

108 / Rhys Davies

Blessed are they who in the Lord are dead,
Though set like Dough, they shall be drawn
like Bread.

What is a cooker without a loving cook? What, that microwave oven without an approach of willing devotion? Even our severely utilitarian and almost foolproof ovens of today, with their marvelous inge-nuities for saving time and temper, ask for that appre-ciative sense of creation I'm sure my aunt felt when she accosted her provider of ever-renewed bliss. After all, apart from that great comfort, the bed, the stove is the most important object in the home. It certainly has a personality of its own, and often approximates human behavior. If treated with contempt, or if looked on as an energy thief, it can retaliate with a bad dish.

Man always felt the need of a cooking stove, and his affinity with it is not likely to leave him. From its beginning as a heap of hot stones in which baked a clay-encrusted bird or, perhaps, a piece of a captured tribal enemy, it has been essential to our well-being and wish for variety. (Look at a man enjoying the recovered satisfaction of barbecue cooking today!) Of course, a stove can be brutally misused to the point where the will to eat is assassinated. The stove has helped to wreck marriages and caused bleak phobias in children. But also it has contributed to the greatness and prosperity of a nation.

We know that France had no culinary reputation until Catherine de Médicis brought Italian cooks to Paris and began that country's long era of treating the stove as of royal importance—a visionary move, both culturally and commercially. The number of foreigners whose initial urge to visit France is the unashamed prospect of a meal must still be enormous. On the other hand, we know that French worship of the stove can be carried to extravagant lengths. In the vast list of French gourmets there was the bland Alexandre Dumas, with his receipt for cooking young elephant's feet and his "soak 15 young shark stomachs for twenty-four hours"—an outrageous glutton who did not stop short at eating donkey. The French had, too, the illustrious Vatel, the chef who committed suicide because he failed the Prince de Condé in a little matter of fish for the king's dinner.

England lagged, and still rather lags, in recognition of the stove as a friendly confederate of man's pleasures. Did Puritanism bring this shunning? There's a nutshell jibe, attributed to Prince Caracciolo, that England has "sixty religions and one sauce." Hawthorne, in 1858, was less impatient: "I doubt whether English cookery, for the very reason that it is so gross, is not better for man's moral and spiritual nature than French." We must allow that, while France was eating, hordes of adventurous men left England and colonized the greatest Empire in the world, though it is far-fetched to assume that the cooking stove drove them from their native hearths.

In the ordinary home the stove is still too exclusively a woman's possession. Surely all men should learn to conquer it, along with their prospective wives? Not only is there the advantage of the husband having independency in time of trouble, but the possibly grateful wife will not feel so victimized by her daily routine. Utopian though it may seem, cooking should be as mutual as other manifestations of conjugal affection. After all, the most celebrated victors of the stove have been men—no doubt due, at least partly, to their being less prone to uncontrolled emotional turmoil. Cooking needs the cool precision of surgeons. A housewife's howl of anguish or venomous curse over a spoiled dish (probably she is thinking of her dear ones) is simply true to her feminine nature.

Then we have that breed of professional women cooks traditionally given to choler and terrible displays of rage. As were queens in history, they are either much loved or much feared. Timid they seldom are. I can remember two such tempestuous ministers.

During the war I was calling at a village policeman's cottage when a locally employed cook arrived with her packed suitcase. She was in boiling condition and denounced her mistress to the policeman. Food rationing was at its most severe just then, and the mistress was obtaining unlimited goods in the black market. But the revelation by this real prima donna of the oven was not prompted by patriotism. Her tirade over, she wept and, pacified by the policeman's tactful wife, admitted that her basic grievance was her employer's refusal to replace a troublesome old range with a modern stove. Her wail simmered down to this: "She dresses fit to kill, eats like a horse, but she won't spend a penny on a new cooker." The moral: give your cook the latest model if you want her to purr.

The other example was a Scotswoman in London who, though obtained from a respectable agency and given an unimpeachable stove, must have had affiliations with the baleful trio of witches in *Macbeth*. I was one of four guests when she sent to the table a dish of beans with a large dead cockroach laid prominently on top. The hostess looked melancholy; her explanation was that the cook's lover, a driver on the underground, had abandoned her.

Such cooks disgrace their sacred workbench. Their behavior indicates that there is room for psychiatrists specializing in neuroses derived from even the labor-saving stoves the manufacturers now shower on us. Mrs. Beeton, that great Victorian crusader for the potentialities of the stove, that august British grandmother of such privileges as we now enjoy from the inescapable domestic object, would not have minced her words about such antics. *She* looked at a suckling pig, took it to the stove with a calm and holy sense of creation, and the pig became poetry.

An official halo has yet to be given to a cook. St. Lawrence and his gridiron, once the emblem of a guild of Paris chefs, had no kitchen status except that the martyr is reputed to have cried out bitterly to the judge watching his torments, "I am roasted enough on this side; turn me round and eat." But I know of one talented lady who, I feel, now enjoys heavenly perfection. Adelaide was the undaunted cook at a boys' charity orphanage and waged ceaseless warfare with the matron, an austere woman given to cheese-paring economies. Adelaide usually won; the orphans, love-children for the most part, were given imaginative meals. In particular she insisted on producing edibles appropriate to numerous saints' festivals, some of them obscure or celebrated only locally—a subtle move in her warfare, since the orphanage was of religious guardianship. The boys ate St. Bride bannocks on the first day of spring, and the feast of St. Catherine found them wolfing what Adelaide called

Cattern cake: treats not given even at Eton. Childless Adelaide also encouraged them to learn the marvels of her trade. One day, too, a hotly pursued little delinquent ran into her kitchen for sanctuary; she hid him in one of the ovens which was capacious as her heart. Her old boys remember Adelaide fondly.

When I asked the domestic science mistress of a primary school if education at the stove included lessons in appreciation of our loyal friend's civilizing, poetic, moral and even humorous values, such as Mrs. Beeton (in the original full editions of her book) and the famous if sometimes besotted French writers have blessed us with, she replied, "No." The girl pupils were only taught how to prepare and cook the mundane everyday dishes. This seems to me shortsighted; it will not help to overcome the still too general English and American attitude toward the stove's greater luxuries and pomps as something faintly reprehensible. She told me, however, that her school was experimenting—a good step forward—with inviting boys to take evening classes in cooking. The response had been gratifying, though the boys, so far, tended to treat the stoves as a means of rewarding them with particular dishes for which they personally were avaricious. But, unlike the girls, they always proudly and delightedly bore their products to her to sample. She agreed that their creative instinct was stirred, as it is in such satisfactions as painting or constructional mechanics.

"The discovery of a new dish does more for the happiness of man than the discovery of a star." Brillat-Savarin's pronouncement might not get a nod of agreement from nations bent on reaching the planets. But it should not be forgotten when next we acquire a new stove. The makers encourage us with the enticing array of gleaming and dextrous models we see waiting in the showrooms, like actresses in the wings. Those stoves will not respond with their best performance if we fail to respect their true worth or feel they demand martyrdom from us.

THE LIGHT BULB

DOM MORAES

To arrive in a city by night is an experience that
always gives me (visa-hardened, magazine-enclosed
traveler though I think myself) a unique and particular thrill. As the airplane, after long hours of sailing
over a blackness total as prehistory, dips its wings and
drones downward and suddenly tier upon tier of
lights swing into view, my neuroses, or most of them,
die away. Even though I know the city beneath me,
and know that I will be bored in its bars, cheated by
its cabmen and misinformed by everyone I interview,
all fears fade before the million fallen stars, scattered
upon the dark, that constitute a human city by night.

Prehistoric man, I often think (assuming, momentarily, that I am civilized), must have had exactly the same feelings when, slinking through black, forested ravines, ears cocked for the rustle of the tiger, he saw, flickering on a faraway hillside, the smudgy campfires of his tribe. For in some degree we all fear darkness. A child is terrified of being left alone at night; many adults repress, not without difficulty, a similar terror. Darkness is not our element: in it, inexplicable shapes swim free.

"Fifteen apparitions have I seen," wrote W. B. Yeats, "the worst a coat upon a coat hanger." Most people have seen similar apparitions in the night. We exorcise them, nowadays, by flicking a switch. A few thousand years ago, the ceremony of exorcism was less simple. Huddled together for warmth in their unlit burrows, our hairy, odorous, uninformed fathers propitiated the darkness with singularly dreadful sacrifices. The sun, the sole purveyor of light, loomed over their religions. Gradually man developed enough common sense to make fire, build settlements by rivers and cultivate the land. Then writing developed, and civilization began.

But the principle of light was still, and has always

been since, the principle of religion. God manifested himself to Moses from a burning bush. Surya and Agni, the gods of the sun and fire, flared over India and Ra over Egypt, before Greece and Rome had begun. The Greeks and the Romans also had their gods of light: St. Paul spoke of the way of light, as opposed to the way of darkness, and in tiny uncivilized corners of the globe the Druids and the Aztecs, until a comparatively recent date, still happily disemboweled youths and virgins in honor of the sun.

The world heaved itself around like a whale through the years, and more ways of providing light were found. Michelangelo, Shakespeare and Dante had literally to burn the midnight oil. Tennyson wrote by gaslight. With the discovery of sources of light more stable than firewood, the old fear of darkness became somewhat sublimated. Electricity was discovered. Then, in 1841, an American engineer aptly called Starr invented the carbon filament lamp. Swan and Edison perfected this in 1878. In these lamps the bulb was drained of air (nowadays it is filled with argon gas) and a carbon filament, introduced into the vacuum, was heated to incandescence by an electric current. General Electric Corporation, already bestriding the light market like a colossus, discovered in 1906 that tungsten filaments provided four times as much light as carbon. All over the civilized world, as a final protection against darkness, men proceeded to fasten a new household god to a wire, swaddle it in a colored skirt and suspend it from the ceiling. There it hung, the dumb herald of the twentieth century. Neon pantheons rose above the cities of the West: divinities of light, shaped like automobiles and bottles of orangeade.

Today, the lights have spread to the cities of the East: Tokyo, Manila, Bombay, Singapore scatter the lurid flicker of neon into the tropical night. For the first time the production of light is unaccompanied by either sound or smell. Fire, candles, oil lamps, gaslights—all crackled, hissed, or sputtered, and each diffused an individual, not always delightful, odor. It is instructive, therefore, to reflect that within fifty years of the introduction of a soundless, odorless source of light, the great capitals of the world are more noisy, and the air more polluted, than ever before in history. You can't, I suppose, win all the time.

Among those of us who move through the thundering streets and the smoky air, different people react differently to different kinds of light. Politicians and businessmen happily scald themselves under long tubular fluorescent lights, filled with mercury vapor. I find that fluorescent lighting—the kind that floods down to reveal not only the geography but the history of the faces beneath—always recalls to me the boring and sometimes horrifying hours I spent in a courtroom in Jerusalem during the Eichmann trial. And the sight of an overhead light always brings me an image of the reception chambers of the Gestapo and the OGPU.

At one time, indeed, I developed a prejudice against electricity which led me into several difficult situations. On the northern border of India, some years ago, I had the choice of staying in a modern hotel or in a resthouse faintly but picturesquely illumined by kerosene lamps. I scorned the hotel, and spent an evening writing by the kerosene lamp. This gave me an insight into the practical difficulties writers must have had before the invention of electricity, and also nearly ruined my eyes forever. Moreover, the lamp attracted an inordinate number of small black insects. I do not know what they were but they were definitely equipped with stings. Next day my face was twice its normal size, and I moved to the hotel.

This experience did not entirely daunt me. A few months later I was thrilled to discover that some friends of mine had moved into a house in central London distinguished by the fact that it was the only house in central London that had never had electricity. I visited it one evening, and was invited to inspect it by the light of an oil lamp. Perhaps I was drunk, otherwise I would not have accepted, in which case I would not have fallen precipitately down two flights of stairs, shattering the lamp and setting the carpet on fire. It was after this incident that I, with some depression, decided that I was after all a creature of the twentieth century. Still, I don't think there is any doubt about the peculiar charm of firelight and candlelight. Despite their incendiary qualities, candles emit a lulling, stroking luminosity that is exceptionally relaxing. In this glow beautiful women expand, just as, by firelight, they take on some of the physical aspects of those cats that spiritually they so much resemble. Electric light lacks this soothing property.

Perhaps the liking expressed by many people nowadays for firelight and candlelight is a specifically contemporary phenomenon. Fires, after all, are now a luxury rather than a necessity. Besides, I think that since the invention of electric lighting, the relationship between man and light has radically altered. The ancient writers saw light as the desirable opposite to an undesirable darkness. Hell, for them, was a dark place. But modern writers, more and more, are coming to see hell as a place that is endlessly floodlit, as Sartre does in *Huis Clos*. Is it because, now, one cannot, in a city, escape from light? Driving toward London in the night, one sees the glow of millions of lights reflected in the sky long before one reaches the city. There is an air of inferno about it. Yet I always recall, when I see the city like this, the other view coming down out of the sky: those miles of spilt stars, signaling the presence of men.

So my moods fluctuate: there are times when I say rude things about Edison under my breath. There is nothing worse than falling heavily and completely asleep after a bibulous party and awaking at some barbarous time in the small hours with a splitting headache and the unextinguished light scorching into your eyes. Firelight is what I crave then, and Alka-Seltzer. At other times, watching traffic lights flick from red to green, or, from a train window, looking out at the cubes of light that are windows, each leading into an individual life and history, I think of electric light as something beautiful, a kind of Morse code of humanity flashed between people who do not know each other and never will.

I often wonder what it would be like if the lights all over the world were suddenly to go out forever. I do not mean this metaphorically at all, but perfectly literally. If, at night, every night, we were faced by the total darkness our forefathers faced—if, like them, we were to kindle small fires, light tapers and oil lamps, and peer from the flickering circle of illumination they afforded at the utter darkness beyond, I think very soon a quiet madness would overtake us all. People would begin to sacrifice babies on the plinth of Cleopatra's Needle, by the Thames.

Ritual murders would take place on the top floor of the Empire State Building. The market workers in Les Halles would demand that de Gaulle should offer his throat to his successor's knife on the first day of the harvest.

Light, in a way, is sanity. You let yourself into your home at night, and your first, automatic gesture is toward the light switch. I have seen a calm and reasonable man, doing this and finding that the light would not go on since the fuse had blown, fly into a fury that was partly panic. Then both of us rushed out into the serene, lamplit street, unable to bear that dark in which ghosts might be gibbering. It was an unreasonable reaction, but I think a natural one. It was as if we had gone into the park and found that all the grass had vanished overnight. For electric lighting has become part of our landscape: its very artificiality has become natural. The great sword of hanging lights that is Sydney Bridge by night is as much a part of the harbor as the water. Conversely, I think the effect of sunlight breaking through the stained glass windows of a cathedral, although unbelievably beautiful, is unbelievably artificial. I have often tried to imagine the effect of a stained-glass light bulb.

This week London has been overtaken by autumn. The trees undress with celerity, there is mist, there are misty bonfires of leaves under a crowded sky. Autumn has always depressed me intensely, for I dislike *la poésie du départ*. Coming home at evening, through the blurred streets, I am filled with macabre fantasies. This is Jack the Ripper's weather, and the season most preferred for European wars. My key turns in the lock; the house is dark inside. But my fingers find a switch, and suddenly the house is lit. Although the English sun has gone on six months' holiday, a constellation of small suns glitters in every room. Books, pictures and furniture are fixed in their identities and places. It is comfortable in here. A midget sun stands over me, and the bogeys of the world and weather retreat through the windows.